Welsh History

A Concise Overview of the History of Wales from Start to End

© Copyright 2019 by Eric Brown - All rights reserved.

The following eBook is reproduced below with the goal of providing information that is as accurate and reliable as possible. Regardless, purchasing this eBook can be seen as consent to the fact that both the publisher and the author of this book are in no way experts on the topics discussed within and that any recommendations or suggestions that are made herein are for entertainment purposes only. Professionals should be consulted as needed prior to undertaking any of the action endorsed herein.

This declaration is deemed fair and valid by both the American Bar Association and the Committee of Publishers Association and is legally binding throughout the United States.

Furthermore, the transmission, duplication or reproduction of any of the following work including specific information will be considered an illegal act irrespective of if it is done electronically or in print. This extends to creating a secondary or tertiary copy of the work or a recorded copy and is only allowed with an expressed written consent from the Publisher.

All additional rights reserved.

The information in the following pages is broadly considered to be a truthful and accurate account of facts, and as such any inattention, use or misuse of the information in question by the reader will render any resulting actions solely under their purview. There are no scenarios in which the publisher or the original author of this work can be in any fashion deemed liable for any hardship or damages that may befall them after undertaking information described herein.

Additionally, the information in the following pages is intended only for informational purposes and should thus be thought of as universal.

As befitting its nature, it is presented without assurance regarding its prolonged validity or interim quality. Trademarks that are mentioned are done without written consent and can in no way be considered an endorsement from the trademark holder.

Table of Contents

Introduction 6
Chapter 1: The Emergence of Wales as A Country 7
Chapter 2: The Defining of Wales 8
    Ancient Wales 8
    Wales in The Middle Ages 10
    In The 16th Century And 17th Century of Wales 13
    Wales in the 18th Century 15
    Wales in the 19th Century 16
    Wales in the 20th Century 17
    The Urge to Unity 19
    The Viking Challenge 20
    The Law of Wales 20
    Relations with England 21
    Urbanism, Architecture, and the Use of Space 23
Chapter 3: The Rise of national consciousness 25
    The Truth of Welsh Nationality in The Mid-
    Nineteenth Century 26
Chapter 4: The Transformations Its People Experienced
and Survived Throughout the Centuries 27
Chapter 5: The Dramatic Conversions Wrought By
The Industrial Revolution 30
    The ascent of vote hyphenated system 32
Chapter 6: Fascinating Things About Wales 33
Chapter 7: Welsh Economy 41
Chapter 8: The History of Welsh Devolution 44
    Early Days 44
    Post-War Wales 45
    Devolution Referendum: 1979 45
    Devolution Referendum: 1997 46
    Welsh devolution – "a procedure not an occasion." 46
    The primary decade, and a changing structure 47

   2011 Referendum Onwards 48
   Welsh devolution – the long view 49
Chapter 9: Timeline of Wales 51
   Timeline 52
   Timeline of Wales 53
Chapter 10: Wales History Map: Wales: First Industrial Nation 54
   National Slate Museum 54
   National Wool Museum 55
   Big Pit National Coal Museum 56
   Blaenavon Ironworks 56
   Pontcysyllte Aqueduct 57
Chapter 11: Welsh Culture: Facts and Traditions 58
   Welsh Culture 59
   Language 59
   National Symbols 59
   Welsh Flags 60
   Family and Religion 60
   Welsh Festivals and Traditions 61
   Family Values and Cultural Communities 61
   Food, Sport, and Attire 62
   Food and Drink 63
   Dress 63
   Sports 63
   Political Life 64
   Social Welfare and Change Programs 66
Chapter 12: Gender Roles and Statuses 67
   The Relative Status of Women and Men 67
   Socialization 68
   Higher Education. 69
   Religion 69
   Rituals 71
   Medication and Health Care 71
   Common Celebrations 72

Chapter 13: The Arts and Humanities 73
   Support for the Arts 73
   Literature 73
   Performance Arts 74
Chapter 14: Description of significant historical places 75
   Kidwelly Castle 75
   Cyfarthfa Castle Museum and Art Gallery 76
   The Six Bells Miners Memorial 77
   Strata Florida Abbey (Cadw) 78
   Oyster Mouth Castle 78
   The Copper Kingdom Center, Amlwch 79
   Caerphilly Castle 79
   Blaenavon has a pretty fantastic story 80
Chapter 15: Welsh Key Figures 82
   Roald Dahl 82
   Aneurin Bevan 83
   Richard Burton 85
   King Arthur Biography 89
   T.E. Lawrence Biography 92
Conclusion 94

Introduction

Britain in the primary Middle Ages was very compared the country it is nowadays. Rather than England, Scotland and Wales, the island contained of many kingdoms, the recognition and affluence of which varied, as some kings increased lordship over others, some smaller kingdoms were believed by their superior neighbors and others fell to foreign invaders – comprising Vikings, in the ninth and tenth centuries.

Today, many of the populations of Britain identify mainly as Scottish, English or Welsh. But this was not continuously the circumstance. In Wales, for instance, there is no solitary defining moment when one can say the people became "Welsh."

In the early Middle Ages, Wales separated into different three kingdoms – Gwynedd, Dyfed, and Ceredigion, for example – whose relations with each other designed a vital plank of native politics.

Chapter 1: The Emergence of Wales as A Country

Wales, constituent unit of the United Kingdom that forms a westward extension of the island of Great Britain. The capital and primary commercial and financial focus are Cardiff.

Celebrated for its strikingly robust landscape, the small country of Wales—which involves six distinctive regions —was one of Celtic Europe's most important political and social focuses, as it holds aspects of culture that are uniquely different from those of its English neighbors.

Chapter 2: The Defining of Wales

Between AD 650 and 750, Britain's lowland zone turned out to be immovably English. Indeed, even in southern Scotland, a large portion of the Brythonic and Welsh kingdoms went under English or Anglian control. However, before that occurred, those kingdoms delivered the first surviving body of literature in the Welsh language, specifically the Gododdin of Aneirin.

The English development squeezed especially hard on Powys. Powys is a principal area and county, and one of the preserved counties of Wales. It is named after the Kingdom of Powys which was a Welsh successor state, petty kingdom and principality that emerged during the Middle Ages following the end of Roman rule in Britain. The Heledd poem is an excellent lament on that kingdom's adversities.

On achieving the Welsh mountains, English development turned into a spent power, a reality which Offa, King of Mercia, perceived. There is proof that, in around 780, he ordered the building of a dike from ocean to ocean. The result was Offa's Dyke, the most critical landmark built in Britain in the second 50% of the first Christian millennium, went far in characterizing the region of Wales.

Ancient Wales

During the last ice age, individuals chased reindeer and mammoth in what is currently Wales. When the ice age finished around 10,000 BC, new animals such as the red deer and wild bear showed up in Wales. Stone Age seekers chased them both as well as gathered plants for food.

In around 4,000 BC, cultivating was brought into Wales, even though the general population still used stone tools. Around

2,000 BC, individuals figured out how to use bronze. At that point, around 600 Celts moved to Wales, carrying iron tools and arms with them. The Celts were warlike persons, and they constructed many slope poles crosswise over Wales. They were also talented; they were skilled craftsmen with iron, bronze, and gold.

In 43 AD the Romans attacked Southeast England. They moved to attack Wales around 50 AD, but the conquest took a very long while. In 78 AD the Romans caught Anglesey, the central command of the Druids, the Celtic ministers. They installed a system of forts crosswise over the land to control any resistant Celtic clans. This effectively squashed opposition. Sometimes towns grew up outside the forts as the soldiers provided a market for the citizens goods. The essential Roman town in Wales was Caerwent. By modern standards, such a town appears modest with only a couple of thousand occupants, but towns were small then.

Christianity landed in Wales in the third century, though it was initially repressed. The Roman Empire did not adopt Christianity as its official religion until the fourth century. Perhaps it is unsurprising then that there are records of two men named Julius and Aaron martyred at Caerleon in 304 AD. Mistreatment of Christians declined from then on and ceased nearly altogether in 313.

Anyway, in the fourth century, the Roman Empire went into decay. The last Roman troopers left Britain in 407 AD and the Roman lifestyle slowly evaporated. Wales split into independent kingdoms.

Wales in The Middle Ages

In the interim, the Saxons attacked eastern England. They walked westwards, and by the seventh century AD, they had conquered the outskirts of Wales. Hundreds of years of battling between the Welsh and Saxons pursued.

This warring continued until the ninth century, when the Vikings began their assault of Wales. Anyway, a man named Rhodri ap Merfyn or Rhodri Mawr (Rhodri the Great) progressed toward becoming ruler of Gwynedd in the northeast. In 855 he also proceeded toward becoming lord of Powys in eastern Wales. In 856 he prevailed upon an extraordinary triumph the Danes. Anyway, the Vikings kept on assaulting Wales, at interims, until the finish of the tenth century.

When William the Conqueror became king of England in 1066 he did not attempt to conquer Wales. Anyway, he granted land along the English-Welsh fringe to Norman masters that impressed him or earned his respect. A few of these masters would later infringe on Welsh land, though not at William's behest.

During the rule of William II (1087-1100), the Normans proceeded with their assaults on Wales. The Welsh opposed sharply, and a large portion of Wales stayed free. In the parts they succeeded in conquering, they created towns, the most imperative of which was Cardiff. The English rulers also established numerous monasteries in Wales.

In the mid-thirteenth century, a man called Llewellyn figured out how to make himself the leader of a large portion of Wales. In 1255 Llewellyn moved toward becoming ruler of Gwynedd. According to the treaty Llewellyn was made Prince of Wales. However he agreed to become the English king's vassal.

In 1272 Edward I progressed toward becoming lord of England. He was resolved to lead all of Great Britain. Since Llewellyn was his vassal, Edward summoned him to do homage. Each time he was summoned Llewellyn made some excuse. In 1276 Edward proclaimed him an agitator and raised a military, which walked into Wales. The next year, Llewellyn was compelled to submit and surrender some of his kingdom to the English. Resentment grew among the Welsh for half a decade until in 1282, they revolted.

Llewellyn was executed battling the English in December 1282, but his sibling Dafyd carried on the fight. Dafyd was caught in June 1283, and he was killed in October 1283. The rebellion was crushed.

Edward became leader of Wales. English law was forced upon the Welsh. Edward constructed a system of castles and installed trusted men to control the general population. Around these castles, villas developed, and out of them, the king made new towns. Nevertheless, the Welsh rose in resistance again in 1294, only the be squashed again in 1295. Yet in 1301 to try and gain the loyalty of the Welsh Edward made his son, who was also called Edward, Prince of Wales.

At that point in 1400, Owain Glyn Dwr drove another resistance. Between 1401 and 1403 the radicals relentlessly progressed, capturing Welsh towns and crushing the English in the fight. In 1404 Owain, took the castles at Aberystwyth and Harlech. The tides began to turn against the Welsh in 1405 and 1406, however, as the English dedicated more resources to the fight and began to recapture lost ground. The English recovered Aberystwyth castle in 1408 and Harlech castle in 1409. Eventually, Owain and his devotees fled to the mountains, but records indicate they continued to battle until 1413. Only then did Owain Glyn Dwr disappear from history— no further mentions are made of him in any written record.

In the late fifteenth century, towns and trade in Wales flourished. Much of the countryside also grew more prosperous. At that point in 1485, Henry Tudor landed with a military at Milford Haven. He walked through Wales into England, after the battle of Bosworth he became king.

The Battle of Bosworth Field was the last significant battle of the Wars of the Roses, the civil war between the Houses of Lancaster and York that protracted across England in the latter half of the 15th century. Fought on 22 August 1485, the battle was won by the Lancastrians.

In The 16th Century And 17th Century of Wales

In 1536 a law divided all of Wales into counties. Wales was to send MPs to the English parliament. A law known as the Act of Union divided Wales into [however many] regions. The sixteenth century also conveyed religious changes to Wales. In 1517 Martin Luther, a German, began the Reformation. He demanded changes in Christian belief and practices.

The Reformation was a movement in Western Christianity in 16th-century Europe. Although the Reformation is usually considered to have started with the publication of the Ninety-five Theses by Martin Luther in 1517, there was no schism until the 1521 Edict of Worms.

In 1536 Henry broke down the smaller monasteries in Wales. The rest were broken down in 1539. In the meantime, Protestant ideas were spreading through Wales. Nonetheless, even though Henry made himself the leader of the congregation, he was not willing to allow numerous changes. In 1542 a Protestant called Thomas Capper was scorched to death in Cardiff.

In 1553 Henry's Daughter Mary moved toward becoming ruler. She endeavored to reestablish the old Catholic faith. During her reign, three Protestants were scorched to death in Wales. When Mary passed just five years later, her sister Elizabeth took the throne and changed the religious landscape once more. Elizabeth I represented Protestantism. In 1588 the Bible was converted into Welsh.

During the sixteenth century, Wales was gradually became more extravagant. A great many people made their living from cultivating, and cow grouping was vital. Exchange and industry kept on developing. Wales exported more and more wool and woolen cloth. Meanwhile coal mining flourished. The Welsh iron industry also grew.

In 1642 came civil war between king and parliament. Wales was firmly in the royalist camp (except for the town of Pembroke which supported parliament all the way through the war) and many Welsh soldiers fought in the king's army. However by 1644 the king was losing the war. In September the royalists were badly defeated at the battle of Montgomery. In 1645 the parliamentary army captured south Wales.

North Wales had been faithful to the lord, but in 1646, parliamentary forces marched on their territory. In 1648 Parliament decided to disband its army. Many fighters had not paid for quite a while, and they realized they would not be paid the money they were owed if they disbanded. The commander of troopers in Pembroke was called Poyer, and he revolted. Meanwhile the king did a deal with the Scots, who guaranteed to reestablish him to his royal position. Poyer put his support behind the ruler, but troopers faithful to parliament Marched to Wales and squashed the resistance.

Wales in the 18th Century

In the mid-eighteenth-century, Wales continued its streak of prosperity, and a number of splendid mansions were built. The SPCK (Society for Promoting Christian Knowledge) established numerous philanthropy schools in Wales. They were given a massive lift by a man named Griffith Jones (1683-1761). He made coursing schools and these were portable schools. Educators would set up a school in one spot for a period between a half year and three years before moving to another location.

Also in the eighteenth century, Wales experienced a religious recovery. In 1735 the Welsh Methodists were founded by Howel Harris (1714-1773) and Daniel Rowland (1713-1790). At first the Methodists remained members of the Church of England but they also held their own meetings. Eventually in 1811, Methodists split and established their own church and clergymen, primarily due to antagonism from ministers of the Church of England.

In the mid-eighteenth century, Wales was still largely a provincial society. Welsh towns were small, even by the standards of the time and vast share of individuals lived in the farmland and lived by cultivating the land. However, toward the end of the eighteenth century, that had begun to change due to the Industrial Revolution, which had people flocking to work in the towns.

Wales in the 19th Century

In the nineteenth-century, coal mining and iron working in Wales boomed. Other metal businesses in Wales, for example, copper, zinc and tin, plating thrived. There was also a vital woolen industry in Wales.

The number of inhabitants in Wales developed quickly notwithstanding displacement. In 1801 the number of inhabitants in Wales was under 600,000. By 1851 it was about 1.2 million. By 1911 it was more than 2 million. Town living became a happy prospect for many Welsh citizens, but by the mid-nineteenth century, they had become overcrowded and grimy. As a result, there were flare-ups of cholera in Wales in 1832, 1848, 1854 and 1866.

There was also turmoil in the Welsh field. There were revolts in the years 1842-1844 known as the Rebecca Riots. The object of their fury were tollgates. (Turnpike Trusts claimed numerous streets in Wales, and you needed to pay a toll to use them).

Later in the nineteenth-century things improved. Wages rose and hours of work were cut. Towns turned increasingly healthy when sewers were burrowed. Moreover during the 1840s railroads were installed crosswise over Wales, which made it a lot easier for guests to visit Wales. The travel industry turned into an essential Welsh industry.

Wales in the 20th Century

The 1920s and 1930s were years of hardship for Wales. There was mass unemployment at that time. Unemployment had already reached 23% of the Welsh workforce in 1927. In the 1930s it grew worse and in parts of Wales half the workforce was unemployed.

Full business came back with the Second World War, but joblessness stayed low through the 1950s and 1960s. Traditional Welsh industries such as coal, iron, and steel-working continued to decline, primarily due to number of collieries were shut.

Luckily new enterprises came to Wales. In 1976 the Welsh Development Agency was shaped to urge industry to move to Wales. The Welsh tourist industry also developed increasingly vital. Other administration businesses also developed insignificance. The number of inhabitants in Wales climbed slowly in the twentieth century significantly more slowly than it did during the nineteenth. Today the number of inhabitants in Wales is 3 million.

In 1999 the Welsh Assembly opened. In 2011 the general population of Wales cast a ballot that the Welsh Assembly ought to be allowed to pass laws without consent from Westminster.

Symbol. The image of Wales, proudly displayed on the flag, is a red dragon. Supposedly brought to the colony of Britain by the Romans, the dragon was a famous image in the ancient world and used by the Romans, the Saxons, and the Parthians. During the War of the Roses, Henry VII flew the red dragon as his fight flag over the fields during the Battle of Bosworth. After his victory and coronation, he proclaimed that it be adopted as the official flag of Wales.

The leek and the daffodil are also critical Welsh images. Some attribute the symbol origin to Saint David, who according to legend defeated the agnostic Saxons over a field of leeks. Almost certainly, leeks were embraced as a national image because of their significance to the Welsh diet, especially during Lent when meat was not allowed.

The Urge to Unity

The presence of Offa's Dyke maybe developed the mindfulness of the Welsh individuals. Inside the age of its development, most of the nation's occupants had turned into the subjects of a solitary ruler.

Rhodri, lord of Gwynedd, had by his passing in 877 added Powys and Seisyllwg (mostly the provinces of Cardigan and Carmarthen) to his kingdom. The union between the North and Seisyllwg ceased with Rhodri's death. It resuscitated by his grandson, Hywel (died 950), who also presided over Dyfed and Brycheiniog.

Dyfed, Seisyllwg, and Brycheiniog were from this point on known as Deheubarth. The process of unity came to a climax under Hywel's great-great-grandson, Gruffudd ap Llywelyn, who by 1057 had united the whole of Wales under his authority.

The Viking Challenge

Rhodri won the designation Mawr (meaning the Great) to a great extent because of his triumph over the Vikings in 856. The Vikings started assaulting the coasts of Britain and Ireland during the 780s. Their assaults on rich and unprotected monasteries helped to decrease the essentialness of the 'Celtic' Church.

In Wales, there is little proof of Viking settlements. However, some towns such as Anglesey, Swansea, and Fishguard were given Scandinavian names. For quite a long time to come, living under the Law of Hywel would be central to what it meant to be a Welsh individual.

The Law of Wales

Welsh law is the main and secondary legislation created by the National Assembly for Wales, using devolved authority granted in the Government of Wales Act 2006 and in effect since May 2007. Each piece of Welsh legislation is known as an Act of the Assembly. The first Assembly legislation to be anticipated was the NHS Redress (Wales) Measure 2008. This was the first time in almost 500 years that Wales has had its own laws, since Cyfraith Hywel, a version of Celtic law, was stopped and replaced by English law through the Laws in Wales Acts, enacted between 1535 and 1542 during the reign of King Henry VIII.

Relations with England

The Viking invasions smashed the state arrangement of the English. Wessex endured and, in the rule of King Alfred, a crusade started to bring the entire of England under the standard of the Wessex dynasty.

Rhodri Mawr died fighting against the English.

Gruffudd ap Llywelyn, on the other hand, was progressively forceful. As a significant aspect of his battle to unite Wales, he seized extensive territories, long lost by the Welsh, to the east of Offa's Dyke. Harold, Earl of Wessex, attacked Wales in 1063 and Gruffudd was chased down and executed. Three years later William, Duke of Normandy, seized the throne of England.

National Identity.

The different ethnic gatherings and clans that settled in ancient Wales gradually consolidated, politically and culturally, to safeguard their region from first, the Romans, and later the Anglo-Saxon and Norman trespassers. The sense of national identity was formed over centuries as the people of Wales struggled against being absorbed into neighboring cultures. The heritage of a common Celtic origin was a key factor in shaping Welsh identity and uniting the warring kingdoms. Cut off from other Celtic organizations toward the north in Britain and Ireland the Welsh clans joined against their non-Celtic adversaries.

The development and continued use of the Welsh language also played important roles in maintaining and strengthening the national identity. The convention of handing down verse and stories orally and the significance of music in everyday

life was critical to the way of life's survival. With the entry of book distributing and an increase in reading proficiency, the

Welsh language and culture could keep on flourishing through the nineteenth century and into the twentieth century, in spite of emotional mechanical and social changes, in Great Britain.

Ethnic Relations. With the Act of Union, Wales increased peaceful relations with the English while retaining their racial personality. Until the late eighteenth century Wales was overwhelmingly rural with the vast majority of the populace living in or around small towns; contact with other ethnic groups was negligible. The Welsh nobility mixed socially and politically with the English and Scottish upper class, creating a very Anglicized top level. The business that grew up around coal mining and steel fabricating pulled in settlers, firstly from Ireland and England to Wales beginning in the late eighteenth century. Poor living and working conditions joined with the entry of vast quantities of immigrants caused social turmoil and often prompted clashes—regularly savage—among different ethnic gatherings. The decay of strong industry in the late nineteenth century caused an outward relocation of Welsh and the nation ceased to pull in foreigners. The modest restoration of industry and the increased standard of living that came with it at the end of the twentieth century brought foreigners back again, though without the violence. Many individuals came to stay, but others came for an excursion; Wales provided an end of the week retreat for people of nearby urban areas in England. Even today, this pattern causes tension in Welsh-speaking, rural areas among occupants who feel that their lifestyle is being undermined.

Urbanism, Architecture, and the Use of Space

The advancement of Welsh urban communities and towns did not start until industrialization in the late 1700s. Rustic areas are portrayed by a dispersement of disconnected ranches, typically comprised of the more seasoned, conventional whitewashed stone structures, usually with slate rooftops. Towns developed from the early settlements of the Celtic clans who picked specific areas for their farming. effective arrangements developed into the political and monetary focuses, first of the kingdoms, and later the individual districts in Wales. The Anglo-Norman manorial custom of structures grouped on a landowner's property, like rural towns in England, was acquainted with Wales after the conquest of 1282. The village as a center of rural society, however, became significant only in southern and eastern Wales; other rural areas maintained scattered and more isolated building patterns. Timber-framed houses, developed initially around an extraordinary hall, rose in the Middle Ages in the north and east, and later all through Wales. In the late sixteenth century, houses started to vary in size and refinement, mirroring the development of a working class and increasing differences in riches. In Glamorgan and Monmouth Shire, landowners constructed block houses that reflected the vernacular style popular in England at the time as well as their social status. This impersonation of English engineering set landowners apart from whatever remained of Welsh society. After the Norman conquest, urban advancement started around castles and military camps. The Bastide, or castle town, even though not expansive, is as yet significant to political and regulatory life. Industrialization in the eighteenth and nineteenth centuries caused an explosion of urban development in the southeast and Cardiff. Lodging deficiencies were average and a few families shared residences. Financial riches and a populace increase created a demand for new development in the late twentieth century. Slightly over 70 percent of homes in Wales are owner-occupied.

In time, however, Wales was in fact subdued and, by the Act of Union of 1536, formally joined to the kingdom of England. Welsh specialists, etymologists, artists, essayists, and fighters proceeded to make significant contributions to the improvement of the more prominent British Empire even as vast numbers of their comrades worked at home to safeguard social customs and even the Welsh language itself, which delighted in a recovery in the late twentieth century. In 1997 the British government, with the help of the Welsh electorate, gave Wales a measure of self-sufficiency through the making of the Welsh Assembly, which is essential leadership specialist for most nearby issues.

Even though Wales was shaken by the decrease of coal mining, before the end of the twentieth century, the nation had built up a diversified economy, especially in the urban communities of Cardiff and Swansea. More rural areas, as mentioned above, drew tourists and retirees from England, turning the travel industry into a financial staple. Guests—including numerous relatives of Welsh—were attracted to Wales' stately stops and castles as well as to social occasions featuring the nation's commended melodic and scholarly conventions. Despite the consistent change, Wales keeps on looking for both more noteworthy autonomy and a particular spot in a coordinated Europe.

Chapter 3: The Rise of national consciousness

Was Welsh nationality perceived in the mid-nineteenth century?

In 1850 there were not many Welsh national organizations. the Calvinistic Methodists had virtually no presence outside of Wales. Meanwhile, the established Church of England comprised of four westerly wards of the Archdiocese of Canterbury, with the Congregationalists and Baptists having virtually no focal association.

The Welsh court system - the Courts of Great Session - was abolished in 1830, making the legal and administrative structure of Wales identical to that of England.

Aside from the Cymmrodorion Society, restored in 1820, and the Cambrian Archeological Society, established in 1847, there were no social or instructive associations at a national dimension, nor did the nation have any financial or expert associations which conveyed its solidarity.

It was commonly accepted that the United Kingdom comprised of three kingdoms: England, Scotland, and Ireland. England was considered to contain the territory of Wales, and the Welsh were considered English. This was a conviction epitomized in the associated flag and the illustrious standard. Generally speaking, any assertions that the United Kingdom consisted of four countries was not well received or supported.

Over the next century, Welsh loyalists succeeded on this point: the idea of four countries gradually supplanted that of three kingdoms.

The Truth of Welsh Nationality in The Mid-Nineteenth Century

While acknowledgment was slight, the substance was specific. The essential marker of the nineteenth century Welsh was language. There existed no registration listing the quantity of Welsh speakers until 1891. However, no less than seventy-five percent of the nation's occupants spoke Welsh in 1850, and a substantial part of that is suspected to have known no other language.

The imperativeness of the Welsh language demonstrated by the number of periodicals distributed in it: in 1866 it was the average used by five quarterlies, 25 monthlies, and eight weeklies, with an entire course of 120,000. Famous books of verse, especially those of Ceiriog, could sell 30,000 copies.

There were also different measurements of Welshness. Welsh religious conventions had unmistakable attributes; provincial settlement designs and tenurial practices were different from those of England; radical developments had very notable highlights; Wales' mechanical networks, a large portion of them situated in the upland nation, were unlike some other. Explorers in Wales, George Borrow pre-famous among them, had presumed that they were in a country of an exceptionally singular character.

Chapter 4: The Transformations Its People Experienced and Survived Throughout the Centuries

A consequence of globalization, new technologies and other factors, the changes in Wales have had profound social and cultural consequences – some of which resemble changes in other areas where there has been a rapid decline of heavy industry, whilst others are distinct to Wales.

To outsiders, it is generally assumed that work in Wales is basically in the overwhelming industries of coal and steel, which has been a fair representation of Wales for quite a long time. Indeed, the workforce crested at 271,000 in 1920. But following the 1984-85 diggers' strike, fuel all but shut down; there are presently no deep pits in Wales, and fuel only utilizes a minor 0.2 percent of the workforce. Steel shut at Shotton in 1980 and Ebbw Vale in 2002, and the steelworks that remain are as profitable as in the past, but with a much-decreased workforce.

At the high-value end of the range are the assembly of the European Airbus wings at Broughton, and vehicle motors at Bridgend, but the broadness of assembling encompasses materials, electronics, car parts, and customer products. Quite a bit of this work includes assembly lines, which is low expertise as opposed to highly valued work. As with elsewhere in the UK, though, work in assembly is in decline, with development occurring in the administration part. Whilst much of this work, in health, call centres, administration and offices is white collar, it has many of the characteristics of blue collar work; and for many it is part-time and even casual.

In the countryside, too, there has been a massive decline in traditional agricultural employment. Milk quotas, BSE then foot and mouth all took their toll on a farming system that is characterized by relatively small units that neither achieve the necessary economies of scale nor benefit greatly from the EU's Common Agricultural Policy. With food makers crushed by the ground-breaking general stores, strategies today incorporate the consolation of diversification and stewardship of the wide open.

In attempting to reinforce the economy, the Welsh Government faces a tough task. In Wales, profitability is low in terms of the Gross Domestic Product (GDP), the estimation of the merchandise and ventures that created per a head. It is because the GDP is quite low – under 75 percent of the EU standard – that a lot of Wales qualifies for EDF Convergence financing.

Another issue is that a significant extent of the populace is economically dormant – higher than in other countries of the UK. Wages are low, and the hole with the UK average pay has not been improving in recent years.

Cardiff is a somewhat different story. Albeit different areas of Wales (counting Monmouth shire and the Vale of Glamorgan) are relatively affluent, there has been an enormous development of work in Cardiff – in government, the media and other associated businesses – especially since the landing of devolution in 1999. In Cardiff today, joblessness is 4.8 percent, contrasted and 14 percent in Merthyr Tydfil and a Welsh average of 9 percent. These figures mask massive amounts of unemployment among youthful individuals from the workforce.

These changes have significant social outcomes. Frequently today, two grown-ups in a family need to work, and the feminization of the workforce has affected traditional gender roles. The reduction in skilled jobs in heavy industries and manufacturing is connected with declining levels of trade union membership as well as lower wages. The convergence of work on the A55 and M4 corridors gives these areas altogether different attributes from west Wales or the South Wales Valleys. The decrease of rural business has had significant ramifications for the maintainability of provincial networks, which have been so vital for the Welsh language and the country lifestyle.

All of these changes in the organization of work and the structure of the economy can be identified in the everyday life of households, with transforming relations of gender and generation shaped in part by the world of work. They relate closely to the distribution of income and wealth and patterns of inequality. They shape the health of the nation, and are the main driver of policies on education. Studying the world of work—in Wales and elsewhere – can lead us to a better understanding of numerous key areas of social life.

Chapter 5: The Dramatic Conversions Wrought By The Industrial Revolution

The Welsh economy in the mid-eighteenth century
In 1750, Wales was still an overwhelmingly rural nation. Its populace of around 500,000 had an expanding modern base.

In the mid-eighteenth century, there were substantial increases in iron making in Pontypool and Bersham, lead, and silver mining in Flintshire and Cardiganshire, copper purifying in Neath and Swansea and coal mining in West Glamorgan and Flintshire.

By the by, they stayed negligible in correlation with the rural economy. That economy was also developing, with the adoption of crop rotation, the use of lime, the enclosure of waste land and the development of proto-industrial production, especially in the woollen industry.

By 1851, Wales was the world's second driving modern country, behind England.

The modern take-off
The take-off into self-supported development happened in the second half of the eighteenth century. However, advancement ought not to originated before. The provinces of Wales separated into hundreds; there were 88 in all and, as late as 1811, 79 of them had a more significant part of occupants still dependent upon the dirt for their employment.

By 1851, 66% of the groups of Wales were upheld by exercises other than farming, which implies that, after the English, the Welsh were the world's second mechanical country.

It was north-east Wales which built up the best scope of ventures. By the late eighteenth century, there were 19 metal works as well as a number of cotton factories at Holywell, and there were 14 potteries at Buckley. Of course, lead and coal mines still proliferated. Bersham, where the Wilkinson family were pioneers in the use of coke as opposed to charcoal in the purifying of iron, was one of Europe's driving ironworks.

By 1830 Monmouth Shire and East Glamorgan were delivering a large portion of the iron sent out by Britain.

In the long haul, the improvements in the southeast were progressively critical. The hearth of Merthyr Tydfil - Cyfarthfa and Dowlais specifically - offered to ascend to Wales' first modern town. By 1830 Monmouth Shire and East Glamorgan were delivering a large portion of the iron traded by Britain.

Monetary advancement was also significant in the Llanelli-Swansea-Neath territory, in Amlwch with its vast copper mine, in Snowdonia where slate quarrying overtook copper mining, and in parts of focal Wales where plant strategies were supplanting household creation in the woolen business.

The ascent of vote hyphenated system

The political representation of Wales before the Reform Act

The Act of Union allowed Wales 27 Members of Parliament, a number that stayed unaltered until the Reform Act of 1832.

In the county constituencies, the vote was vested in freeholders owning land worth £2 a year; in the boroughs it was the burgesses who were generally the voters. Both the county and borough systems were open to manipulation by landed families.

There were few genuine freeholders and most county voters were enfranchised through leases granted to them by their landlords. Almost all boroughs were controlled by estate owners and it is they who decided who became burgesses.

By the late eighteenth century, a tight gathering of somewhere in the range of 20 families controlled the parliamentary portrayal of Wales.

The framework in Wales was less immoral than it was in England. There were no completely rotten boroughs, fewer towns with no representation at all, and the inequality between the counties was not as blatant.

Nevertheless, with voting a public act, less than 5% of adult males enfranchised, bribery rampant and estate owners virtually the only moneyed class, landlord dominance of the electoral process was inevitable.

It was generally chosen not by the casting of votes, but by private courses of action which guaranteed the rise of a solitary unopposed candidate. In the general race of 1830, for instance, not one of the Welsh supporters was challenged.

Chapter 6: Fascinating Things About Wales

Though many have heard about Welsh mines and the immense cathedrals planted over its rolling green hills, there are lesser known points that are just as captivating things from Welsh history that haven't instructed in schools.

They each tell a story about Wales at a particular time (and those times range from the prehistoric to the 20th century).

The vast majority of information comes from eminent Welsh historian John Davies' epic work, A History of Wales.

The banks of the Taff once had fortifications to prepare for assaults by the Irish
The Irish were a threat to Roman Britain. Fortresses were built along the River Taff and heavily guarded in order to prevent their crimes. Settlements of Irish existed in Wales long after the Romans. Names, for example, Llyn and Dinllaen are of Irish birthplace, as was the kingdom of Dyfed, where there are 20 stones engraved with letters in ogham from Ireland.

Vikings sold the general population of Wales as slaves
The Vikings more than once assaulted Wales in the tenth century. They attacked villages and town all along the coast from their fortresses on the Isle of Man and in Dublin. It's most likely in this time Scandinavian names, later embraced in English, were given to places like Swansea, Bardsey, Anglesey, and Fishguard. They built up small exchanging stations in Cardiff.

A saint was burned at stake for heresy in Cardiff
Thomas Capper's life "ended" Cardiff in 1542 when he was burned alive. He was a Protestant and the chief religious saint in Wales since Roman Times, a casualty of Henry VIII's

oppression of the individuals who precluded from Catholic mass.

These were at one time the 'four capitals' of Wales

According to John Davies, Carmarthen, Caernarfon, Denbigh, and Brecon were once the four capitals of the four corners of Wales. Carmarthen was the most populas town in Wales in the sixteenth century with around 2,000 individuals. The other three had about each 1,000. By 1700, Wrexham was the biggest town in Wales, but Carmarthen had restored its lead by 1770.

The first word of wales

Although Welsh may have been recorded in writing as early as 600 [AD?], the first surviving words are found on a stone in a congregation in Tywyn, and they date from around the year 700. Early Welsh was the mechanism of Taliesin and Aneirin, writers of the time. It is especially significant as Latin was the primary written language throughout Europe and there was virtually no composed French, Spanish or Italian until after 1000. The adoption of the word 'Cymru' may have been around the same time, with the word 'Kymry' used in a poem from 633. Around then, the word alluded to the Old North as well as to Wales.

There were no less than 5,000 Mormons in Wales around 1850

A Wales native named Daniel Jones migrated to America in 1840, where he converted to the Church of Latter-Day Saints. When he returned to Wales in 1845, he set up a church in Merthyr and there converted over 5,000 individuals. The religious registration of 1851 records 28 Mormon assemblages in Wales. In 1849, 326 Welsh Mormons migrated to Salt Lake City, presently the world capital of Mormonism. in 1949 there were 25,000 Mormons of Welsh descent in America.

When 'the first Welshman' lived

Human teeth have been found in Wales dating to 225,000 years back. Even though these have been portrayed as having a home with 'the first Welshman,' their proprietor was unlikely to be a progenitor of the Welsh. Instead, he or she was likely apart of a Neanderthal…" There were a considerable number of years since during which Wales was utterly uninhabited, including an ice age. Ridges was free of ice by 8,300BC. When that occurred, Wales "become" a piece of an island and an ocean, not a strait, isolated from Ireland.

Every bank in Pembroke shire flopped in 1825

In 1825, a financial emergency was declared due to [reason]. This lead to the shutdown of many—if not most—Welsh banks that had been established in market towns before 1770. These incorporate all the banks in Pembroke shire. numerous ranchers "lost" their investment funds. The circumstances at the time inspired revolts in the field, including at Carmarthen, Abermule, and Maenclochog.

There were harsh dissents against the Irish crosswise over Wales

In 1851, around 20,000 individuals in Wales had been born in Ireland. They were in anxious conditions and therefore arranged to work for wages lower than the Welsh. Thus there were "severe challenges" against them. These occurred in

Swansea in 1828, in the Rhymney Valley in 1825 and sporadically elsewhere. Irish lived in ghettos, and John Davies wrote that "the conviction emerged that uncleanliness and boisterousness were a natural piece of their character."

A home in England is to thank for The national song of devotion

When Wlad Fy Nhadau was written in 1856 by Evan and James of Pontypridd, but it only because of the National Eisteddfod in Chester in 1866 that it turned into the national song of praise. It was sung with such passion that it promptly was embraced as an athem. A guest to that expressed: "When I see the enthusiasm which these Eisteddfods stir in your entire individuals I am loaded up with profound respect."

In Blackwood in 1842, there was one bar for Every five individuals

After the Beer Act of 1830, there was a tremendous increase in the quantity of spots individuals could go for a drink. there were 200 bars around the Dowlais Ironworks alone. alone. It was not long for laws to be passed to curb the excessive drinking. The first teetotal society in Wales established in Llanfechell, Anglesey in 1835. A survey in Mountain Ash professed to have set up that 90% of individuals supported shutting bars on Sundays.

In 1603 there were around 18 schools in Wales

Grammar schools for the less wealthy were established in Welsh market towns (though you could find Welsh pupils at Eton and Westminster). They were established to teach the basics of Latin. Welsh was not tolerated in the schools - it was deemed irrelevant to ambitions in the gentry and a career.

The termination of the Welsh language predicted in 1682

William Richards prophesized the inevitable demise of the Welsh language. Bardic schools were failing, parents no longer gave their children Welsh names and many customs were being looked at as meaningless. In the meantime, Thomas Jones went further, anticipating that Welsh individuals would be "expunged from history." The Anglicization of the Welsh upper class was among the underlying drivers. However, this proved to be incorrect thanks to Griffith Jones, a [profession] who set up schools all across Wales in order to ensure the continuation of the Welsh language. In the next 100 years, Welsh could spread quickly. The eighteenth century, Wales was one of only a handful couple of nations with a predominantly educated populace.

Individuals in Haverfordwest were the last individuals to experience the ill effects of the plague

Even though outbreaks of the plague had been substantially reduced in the 16th century, Wales continued to have sporadic outbreaks, like the rest of the UK. There was an occurrence recorded in 1652, but the last was around 1700. Although better treatment was available by that point, the death rate during this particular outbreak was substantial—multiple times more than usual—primarily because of a starving population.

The Law of Wales was relatively revolutionary

It dates to the tenth century, but the Law of Wales took ladies and children into the record in manners that were not found in English law up to this point. The original copy is in Latin, but there are a few duplicates, including those written in Welsh. One example of its fairness is its recognition that the union of a man and woman was a contract and that it could come to an end. Accordingly, it itemized how property and duty regarding children ought to shared if that occurred. It was later condemned as the work of the devil by Canon Law.

Sex outside marriage was a noteworthy issue before the courts

Between 1633 and 1637, a third of the punishments meted out by the Council of Wales related to these offences, which were considered as serious as violence and subversion. Around 10% of childrens brought into the world with only one parent present.

Better food was served in jails than in workhouses for poor people

The years 1834-45 were "among the most agitated ever," wrote John Davies. There was widespread distress and extraordinary destitution and so every one of Wales' 48 "associations" (areas assembled into associations) were obliged to manufacture a workhouse A Poor Law said no one could be helped at home - so they had to move to a workhouse to get help. Married couples were not allowed to go there together - so families were part up. Workhouses were horrendous, and it guaranteed in Carmarthenshire that "individuals wanted to kick the bucket rather than enter it."

The word 'Sais' was first given to a Welshman who learned how to communicate in English

'Sais' is used today in Welsh to portray somebody English, here and there in a deprecatory manner. In any case, it was first used in the fifteenth century to depict a Welshman who knew how to communicate in English. Welsh individuals had little reason to know the language in medieval times, and the use of the word recommends the information was uncommon and viewed with scorn.

A house of prayer was assembled every eight days

Between 1801 and 1851, it is estimated that a chapel was completed every eight days. There were enough chapels in the 19th century to seat half the country's population. A leading Christian historian has claimed religion "had been more successful in retaining the informed allegiance of the mass of the population in Wales than in any other country in Europe".

The Romans thought that it was difficult to curb the general population of Wales

There were at least 13 campaigns between AD48 and 79 and the Romans weren't used to the guerrilla fighters of the Welsh mountains. But they did manage to form a network of forts, with corners at Carmarthen, Caernarfon, Caerleon and Chester.

In 1966 you could head out from Holyhead to Chepstow without leaving a Labor supporters

The Labour party dominated Welsh politics in the 1960s. In 1966, it won 32 of the 36 constituencies, taking Monmouth from the Conservatives and Cardiganshire from the Liberals, who had held it since 1880. You could travel from Holyhead to Chepstow without leaving a Labour constituency, using the ferry from Ynyslas to Aberdyfi.

Jewish shops assaulted in Tredegar in 1911

In 1911, a riot broke out in Tredegar primarily due to anti-Jewish sentiments. Jewish businesses and properties were attacked and damaged, but there were no casualties also spread to places including Bargoed and Brynmawr. It was in the same time as against Semitism in Russia, but there are questions as to whether the attacks in Wales specifically coordinated at Jews. This incident occurred at the same time that antisemitism was on the rise in Russia, but it is questioned whether the attacks in Wales were specifically coordinated against the Jewish.

In 1932, nearly half of Welsh men was jobless

The sorrow that started during the 1920s was "the focal occurrence in the historical backdrop of twentieth-century Wales," Wrote John Davies. Individuals left the nation in huge numbers, and there were fewer individuals remaining in 1931 than in 1921. In 1932, 42.8% of men were out of work. Although the depression affected every developed country "the experience of Wales was exceptional in severity and length". In many nations, it was over by the mid-1930s, but in 1939 there were still 100,000 men out of a job in Wales. In 1926, Coal diggers of South Wales lost a joined £15 million in wages - that is more than £1 billion in today's money.

Chapter 7: Welsh Economy

There is a long-standing joke in Wales that the economy is something of a dinosaur in comparison to whatever remains of the UK's. But even though customary industries like coal mining have decline in Wales, the economy was not disparaged, largely thanks to the success of the tourism industry.

In the 21st Century, where – owing to the recent recession – more and more people are curious about how the UK economy functions, we should investigate a couple of things you might now know about the Welsh economy.

Startup Comes to Wales

A successful Welsh businessman named Tim Morgan pioneered a startup called DeskBeers. The company's objective is to bring specialty lagers to workplaces on Friday afternoons, with the goal being to improve staffers' weeks. Until now, DeskBeers has primarily operated in London, but is currently in development in Wales. It is projected to have a high demand as soon as it begins. More ideas like Tim's, please!

Tourism Is Booming in Wales

If the travel industry in Wales has ever needed a lift, it got a noteworthy one in 2014, when £150 million was siphoned into the Welsh economy to promote popular travel destinations.

This resulted in over 1,000,000 more travelers visiting the nation in 2014 than in 2013, with the travel industry presently immovably observed as a substantial zone of the venture.

One of the First Laser Projection will call Wales home

Truth is stranger than fiction - Premiere Cinemas will assume control over Cardiff's rundown Odeon Film, breathing new life into the city with a groundbreaking film that will be one of the first in the UK to embrace laser projection.

A minimum of 4 screens will be laser, whilst at least one will be 4K quality, emulating Premiere's successful business model throughout the UK.

House Prices Are Low in Wales

Mirroring a UK pattern, of house costs in Wales have been falling gradually for over a year.

This means that more and more mid-market sectors are now being challenged to lower their prices too.

Disinflation in Wales

The prices of goods and services in Wales has fallen to an all-time low, with the Consumer Price Index coming in at 0.5%.

The Euro-zone doesn't want mass-scale flattening, but commentators have acknowledged that the deflation in Wales is much welcomed. Fuel costs have fallen as well, freeing up cash for Welsh citizens to spend on different types of merchandise and luxury goods. Hurrah!

Welsh Economy of North Wales

The success of the North Wales economy is critical to the achievement of Wales, with Welsh Secretary Stephen Crabb watching: "When the North Wales economy is progressing admirably, Wales is progressing admirably."

The point is for an assortment of dynamic and inventive firms in North Wales to be allowed to flourish, with internal speculation depicted as of late as being "extremely useful for Wales."

Lloyds Bank Has the Gay Vote

Stonewall, a group of campaigners and lobbyists for equality and justice for gays, lesbians and bisexuals, placed Lloyds Bank, which has a massive workforce presence in Wales, in the top 10 of their 'best places to work if you are gay' list.

It shows that the correct sort of groundbreaking balance culture is being sharpened at the financial mammoth, prompting efficiency and collaboration. And it's nice to see this is perceived.

Chapter 8: The History of Welsh Devolution

Early Days

The foundations of political devolution in Wales can be traced to the end of the nineteenth century. In 1886, Cymru Fydd ('Young Wales') was set up to advance the destinations of the Liberal Party in Wales and to crusade for Welsh 'home rule.' Even though Cymru Fudd's prosperity was fleeting, its exercises corresponded with other political improvements, including the passing of specifically Welsh Acts without precedent for the UK Parliament. It also compared with the start of administrative devolution in Wales through the Creation of the Welsh Board for Education in 1907.

Post-War Wales

After the Second World War, a Series of improvements began from Westminster to Wales.

Petitions to make a Secretary of State for Wales were turned down by the Labor Government of 1945-50. As a concession, it established a Council for Wales and Monmouth shire in 1948. It was a selected body that advised the legislature on Welsh undertakings.

In 1951, another minor government post of Minister of State for Welsh Affairs was created by the conservative UK government. Initially it was held by a minor clergyman in the Home Office, but from 1957 on, it was a post held mutually with the Ministry of Housing and Local Government.

The Labor Party finally to make a Secretary of State for Wales in its 1959 race manifesto, but it needed to hold up until its triumph in the 1964 UK general decision to formally do the job. At first, the Secretary of State just had duty regarding lodging, neighborhood governments, and streets. Over the years, other areas of responsibility were added, such as health, trade and domestic industry, nature and farming gradually included throughout the years.

Devolution Referendum: 1979

The primary vote on devolution in Wales took place on 1 March 1979. It pursued a Royal Commission on the Constitution in 1973. It detailed the selection of bodies for both Scotland and Wales. The proposition for the output of a Welsh Assembly in 1979 was dismissed by the Welsh Open, who cast a ballot four to one against the UK Labor Government's recommendations.

In the aftermath of the 1979 decision, devolution turned into somewhat of a lethargic political issue in Wales. Be that as it may, the arrangements of the UK Conservative Government during the difficult monetary states of the 1980s, combined with the Conservative Party's moderately low dimensions of constituent help in Wales (in contrast with the UK), prompted restored calls for Wales to have its very own majority rule establishment.

Devolution Referendum: 1997

In May 1997, when Labor suddenly returned to power, its manifesto incorporated a promise to hold a vote on the creation of a Welsh Meeting. A White Paper, A Speech for Wales, was distributed in July 1997. It delineated the UK Government's recommendations and, on September 18, a vote was held.

As the results were announced, constituency by constituency, Wales had to wait for the very last declaration before knowing the final result. Of the individuals who cast a ballot, 50.3 per cent supported devolution – a narrow majority in favor of 6,721 votes.

Welsh devolution – "a procedure not an occasion."

Following the decision, the UK Parliament passed the Government of Wales Act 1998. The Act built up the National Assembly as a corporate body – with the official (the administration) and the lawmaking body (the Assembly itself) working as one.

The first decisions in the Assembly were held on 6 May 1999.

In contrast to the essential law-making powers given to the Scottish Parliament, the Act restricted the National Assembly to the making of auxiliary enactment in specified areas, including horticulture, fisheries, instruction, lodging, and thruways. Such powers were extensively identical to those recently held by the Secretary of State for Wales.

The primary decade, and a changing structure

While there were numerous positives about the Assembly regarding community and a progressively comprehensive and consensual style of political issues, the single corporate body structure proved to be problematic. The difficulties experienced by the minority Labor organization in verifying predictable understanding from different gatherings in the Assembly. The substitution of the First Secretary in February 2000, featured the need for established change and strength.

Because of increased calls for change, the Assembly concurred goals in 2002 to isolate the two jobs as much as conceivable inside the structure of the 1998 Act. It accomplished by presenting the term Welsh Assembly Government to depict the arrangements. Activities of the Cabinet as unmistakable from crafted by the National Assembly, which had more prominent freedom to give counsel, research and backing to singular Members and advisory groups of the Meeting.

The Welsh Government's choices and activities held within proper limits by the National Assembly (an assortment of 60 members which holds its ministers to account. The National Assembly makes laws and speaks to the interests of the general population of Wales.

2011 Referendum Onwards

Following a submission in 2011, the Assembly increased essential lawmaking powers in connection to specific subjects without inclusion from Westminster or Whitehall. The UK Government set up the Silk Commission to consider the eventual fate of the devolution settlement in Wales.

In 2012, the Silk Commission distributed Part I of its report, making suggestions on the money-related forces of the Assembly.

Silk Commission published Part II of its report in 2014, making recommendations on the Assembly's future legislative powers and arrangements.

The UK Government distributed Powers for a Purpose in 2015, providing the basis for the development of a reserved powers model of devolution for Wales.

The assembly passed the Tax Collection and Management (Wales) Act 2016, in anticipation of practicing the tax assessment and getting powers declined by the Wales Act 2014. It saw the beginning of Assembly's job in directing the UK's exchanges for leaving the EU, investigating enactment, and characterizing Wales' place in the post-Brexit UK.

2018 saw the beginning of held forces model of devolution under the Wales Act 2017. The first Welsh taxes came on stream.

In 2019, income tax-varying powers will come on stream, as provided by the Wales Act 2014.

Welsh devolution – the long view

c. 940 Welsh laws united as one code under Hywel Dda (Hywel the Good)

1282 The Edwardian victory of Wales and the end of government by local Welsh sovereigns

1400 Owain Glyndwr's revolt begins and for a brief time builds an early Welsh state. Parliaments are held at Harlech and Machynlleth

1536 The Acts of Union, making Wales a part of England but providing for parliamentary seats for MPs from Wales.

1881 The Sunday Closing Act of 1881 was passed. This was the first law passed by the UK Parliament that pertained to Wales only.

1907 Welsh branch of the Board of Education Was created

1920 The Church of Wales turns into a free body, distinct from the state

1951 Pole of Minister of State for Wales made

1964 Welsh Office set up alongside a bureau post of Secretary of State for Wales

1979 First proposition for a Welsh Assembly turned down in a submission

1997 Wales cast a ballot for making a National Assembly for Wales in a vote.

1999 First races held. The National Assembly begins work. Government of Wales Act 1998 comes into power

2007 Government of Wales Act 2006 comes into effect; the National Assembly and Welsh Government are formally isolated, and the National Assembly picks up forces to make laws for Wales in certain areas

2011 Wales votes in favor of giving the National Assembly further law-making powers

2014 The Wales Act 2014 is passed, the National Assembly advanced law-making controls

2017 The Wales Act 2017 is passed, perceiving the permanence of the National Assembly for Wales and Welsh Government and shifting the model of devolution to an Earmarked Powers Model.

Chapter 9: Timeline of Wales

70 The Romans invade AD Wales

383   The idea of the Welsh country develops when the Picts and Celts attack the land

440   Britain, abandoned by the Romans, passes to the possession" or something of the sort.

784   The King of Mercia fabricates Offa's Dyke as a limit between England and Wales

844   844-877 the reign of Rhodri Mawr (Rhodri the Great) begins and lasts until 877. During it, he unites all of Wales.

890   Welsh lords recognize Alfred of Wessex (Alfred the Great) as their ruler

1066   1066-77 Following the annihilation of the English King Harold at the Battle of Hastings, the Normans assume responsibility for Wales

1120   1120-1129 "Historia Regum Britanniae" was composed by Geoffrey of Monmouth and details the Arthurian Legend of King Arthur. This provided the Welsh with a claim to the sovereignty of the whole island of Britain of which the Tudors took advantage

1137   The Reign of Owain Gwynedd (1137-1170) begins

1169   According to Welsh legend, Prince Madog of Gwynedd, landed in Alabama and went up to Missouri

1204   Prince Llywelyn Ap Iorwerth (1173-1240) wedded Joan, the daughter of King John of England

1240   Dafydd ap Llywelyn (c. 1208 February 25, 1246) was Prince of Gwynedd from 1240 to 1246 who had two children of Gruffydd, Llywelyn ap Gruffydd and Owain ap Gruffydd.

1277   King Edward branded Llywelyn ap Gruffydd "a rebel and disturber of the peace" and declared his lands forfeit

1278   Edward I had propelled a massive invasion of Wales, revanquishing South Wales and overcoming Llywelyn ap Gruffydd and North Wales. Llywelyn ap Gruffydd was compelled to agree to settle for peace of Aberconwy. Edward appointed the construction of four noteworthy castles in Wales - Flint, Rhuddlan, Builth, and Aberystwyth

1282   Llywelyn ap Gruffyd Began second Welsh rebellion with his sibling David. Llywelyn ap Gruffydd was slaughtered in a fight and his sibling David was caught and executed.

1284   Wales wound up consolidated into The Kingdom of England under the Statute of Rhuddlan

1485   The Battle of Bosworth ended the English Wars of the Roses when Henry Tudor crumpled Richard III. Henry Tudor asserted Welsh descent through Owain Tudor of Penmynedd in Anglesey. He had married Catherine, widow of King Henry V. Their child, Edmund Tudor fathered Henry Tudor, who King Henry VII of England and satisfied the old prophesy that one day a Welsh Monarch would control the entire of Britain.

Timeline

The History Timeline of Places, including the Timeline of Wales, gives fast realities and information about this favorite spot with its history. The most important occasions of the nation nitty gritty together with related chronicled occurrences which organized in sequential, or date, request giving a whole succession of times in the Timeline of Wales. The Timeline of Wales provides fast information via this time line which highlights the key dates and events of the famous place in a fast information format with concise and accurate facts and information in the order of their occurrence. The Timeline of Wales incorporates a sequence of this vital spot and its history. Specific data can be seen initially with brief and precise subtleties using the Timeline of Wales. This History course of events of a favorite spot is reasonable kids and incorporate numerous critical occasions of significant event and result which are point by point in the Timeline of Wales.

Timeline of Wales

- Fast and accurate time line details via history timelines and chronologies
- Chronology of Key Names, Key Dates, Key People and Key Events in the Timeline of Wales
- Useful time line database of history and this Timeline of Wales containing interesting chronology of facts & information
- Famous people, famous places and countries and famous events via comprehensive
- Interesting Information via the Timeline of Wales - Time line History and Chronology at a glance, for children and kids
- Chronologies of key dates, facts and info

Chapter 10: Wales History Map: Wales: First Industrial Nation

Wales has a fascinating background more than just in terms of its industrial legacy—it has numerous spots of treasure, which is perhaps why it has become such a popular destination for tourists. However, it is not simply its past that makes it significant; a modern site has garnered such significance that it has been deemed worthy of a World Heritage Marker.the core of the south Wales valleys offers various attractions including the chance to experience life as an excavator at Big Pit National Coal Museum, and as a laborer at the Blaenavon Ironworks. west is home base to the National Wool Museum, situated in the memorable Cambrian Mills, and the core of the Snowdonia mountains in north Wales is the National Slate Museum.

National Slate Museum

The National Slate Museum recounts the narrative of life in Wales' slate networks when the Welsh slate industry 'roofed the world.'

As well as chances to see the shops, fashions, sheds and the most prominent working waterwheel in the UK, talented experts also give live shows of the craft of part and dressing account.

The National Slate Museum is twinned with the Slate Valley Museum in Granville, NY, USA, strengthening the connections between Welsh people group on the two sides of the Atlantic.

National Wool Museum

What? A museum situated inside Cambrian Mills.

Where? Carmarthenshire.

Located in the core of west Wales, the National Wool Museum recounts the tale of the once flourishing-cool industry in Teifi Valley.

This pearl of a museum is housed in a unique plant building, where new apparatus and live weaving showcases can be seen which demonstrate the procedure of 'fleece to fabric.'

Did you know? The fleece business overwhelmed the Teifi zone in the late nineteenth and mid-twentieth.

Big Pit National Coal Museum

What? Industrial heritage museum.
Where? Blaenavon.

At the core of the UNESCO World Heritage landscape of Blaenavon lies Big Pit, a former working coal mine. This award-winning museum offers an experience unparalleled in the nation, and it is one of just two locales in the UK where guests can go underground in a single coal mine.

Guided by ex-diggers, guests plummet to the depths of the mine and experience what life was like for the individuals who made their living at the coal face.

There are further offices to instruct and engage all ages, including a multi-media virtual visit in the Mining Galleries and displays in the unique colliery structures.

Did you know? The open mines at Big Pit lie more than 90 meters underneath the ground.

Blaenavon Ironworks

Just under an hour's drive from Cardiff in the renowned south Wales Valleys stands Blaenavon Ironworks. The ironworks were an achievement of the Industrial Revolution.

The intensity of steam was saddled, and a method for making steel utilizing iron mineral was created, which prompted an overall blast in the steel business, taking Wales' modern way to another stature. Visitors can see the renovated Stack Square cabins, to experience how the workers, survived the ages and the reproduced organization truck shop. New, cutting-edge audio-post technology breathes life into the tale of the Ironworks.

The landscape of Blaenavon has elevated World Heritage status because of its mounting structure and capacity. From mines to prepare lines, you can now follow the courses in and out, from crude material to completed item.

Did you know? Originally built in 1790, people lived in Blaenavon Ironworks's Engine Row cottages until the 1960s.

Pontcysyllte Aqueduct

What? Nineteenth-century water channel.
Where? To Close Llangollen.

The Pontcysyllte Aqueduct directs the Llangollen Canal over the valley of the River Dee in Wrexham County Borough.

Created by Thomas Telford in 1805, it's no exaggeration to state that the systems and ideas created at Pontcysyllte helped shape the world through their impact on engineering. Taking over 10 years to build and costing £38,499 — the equivalent of £38 million today — the Pontcysyllte Aqueduct was truly one of the engineering marvels of the Industrial age. UNESCO made this masterpiece a World Heritage Site in 2009 – alongside 11 miles of waterway including Chirk Aqueduct and the Horseshoe Falls at Llantysilio, to close Llangollen.

Did you know? When Thomas Telford completed the Pontcysyllte Aqueduct in 1805, it was the tallest trench vessel crossing on the planet.

Chapter 11: Welsh Culture: Facts and Traditions

In this section, we will explore Welsh culture Investigate the way of life of land of imaginary dragons, a particular language, passionate games fans, and exciting food. In this exercise, find out about certain aspects of the Welsh culture and also look at certain customs and celebrations.

There is more to Wales than the sports and interesting cuisine. The culture of the Welsh is filled to the brim with mythological dragons and a very elvish language. Many of the cultural practices in Wales is taken from England and adopted to the Welsh lifestyle and beliefs. The little country has managed to keep its culture and traditions intact despite the large influence that its English neighbors have on it.

The nation is said to have had people possessing it for the past 30,000 years. The country was at one time a piece of the Roman Empire, and therefore, there are hints of Celtic roots still mixed in the way of life. If there is a single word to portray Wales, it's Green. Everything from backwoods, mountains, and farmlands are scattered in abundance across the entire country with quaint places for inhabitation by humans.

The Welsh culture is loaded with customs and legends. Indeed, even a dragon is the national image! This nation has embraced numerous social aspects from neighboring England, but despite everything, it keeps its national character and various unique customs.

Wales is a small country situated in the western piece of Great Britain. People are accepted to have lived around there for something like 29,000 years. The Welsh culture has Celtic roots, and the land was once part of the Roman Empire. In the

Middle Ages, it governed by Norman knights and was defeated by England in 1282. When the United Kingdom was built up in 1707, Wales turned out to be a piece of it.

There are vast farmlands, mountains, and woods areas, many ensured as national parks. The populace is more than 3 million, and Cardiff is the capital city and the most significant urban region.

Welsh Culture

The Welsh culture has been influenced by England for centuries, so both share some joint aspects. However, there has always been an interest in preserving cultural elements that make the Welsh unique and significantly different from other cultures in the United Kingdom.

Language

The two official dialects are English and Welsh. There have been endeavors to save the plain Welsh language, and it is now instructed in schools as well as incorporated into printed media and television. Nonetheless, the use of Welsh has gradually decreased and now just around one-fifth of the populace can speak it.

National Symbols

Since medieval occasions, the dragon has been a critical image of Wales. This legendary animal is referenced in several legends and is part of the national flag, which features a red dragon in the middle.

Welsh Flags

Daffodils and leeks are also public images. It trusted that the leek was initially the main image and the daffodil was gradually received afterward. It was most likely because of perplexity between the two words. In Welsh, the leek is cenhinen, and daffodil is cenhinen Bedr (which deciphers as Peter's leek).

Family and Religion

Most of the populace identifies as Christian. The most significant sects in Wales are the Methodists, Presbyterians, Anglicans, and Catholics.

more distant families frequently meet once every week, usually on Sundays after going to chapel. It generally trusted that numerous neighborhood families are connected, so discussions among outsiders regularly incorporate asking about relatives in like manner.

Welsh Festivals and Traditions

Welsh customs are an intriguing blend of old folklore, legends, and religious customs. A portion of the traditional celebrations and festivities are:

- St. David's Day: Considered Wales' National Day, it is celebrated on 1 March to honor the passing of Saint David, the national benefactor holy person. Daffodils and leeks are displayed in numerous spots. Individuals frequently wear common clothing types, wave national flags, and eat typical dishes. A parade is a piece of the festival in countless urban towns.

Family Values and Cultural Communities

The whole nation has a remarkable language which is a long way from the English language that we used. There is a ton of consideration taken to safeguard the first language of the Welsh for its significance and chronicled esteem. The word itself sounds elvish, and you can see it used in numerous mysterious films as well. The quantity of individuals who speak Welsh lacks nowadays. Monsters, daffodils, and leeks are public images based on the legendary legends that structure the core of their custom.

The vast majority in Wales are Christians of different sections. Meeting with more distant families is a critical piece of the way of life and is frequently a custom. After chapel, families get together for dinner and hang out. Kids accordingly grow up to be a piece of the more distant family regardless of whether they live with only their folks. The towns are small, and a great many people know one another. When a more bizarre meets another Welsh individual, they regularly go into nitty-gritty discussion about identifying the family that they originate from, which viewed as weird in numerous traditions.

Food, Sport, and Attire

Since a great deal of Wales engaged with cultivating, their cooking is frequently, meat-based but has a ton of vegetables as well. Wales has a significant portion of long, craggy coastlines, which provides them with seafood. Their stews and soups are fantastic. The liquor delivered locally and mainly comprises of Whiskey and Beer.

The customary clothing of the Boast. The ladies occasionally wear long red and white checkered dresses covered with a frilled white apron. A tall, dark cap compliments the clothing. Some parts of Wales still have ladies who dress in conventional clothing, but the vast majority of Wales has begun wearing typical Western apparel.

If you are a sports fan, it is likely you may know about the Welsh rugby group. Passionate players play the game, and local people are equally enthusiastic about supporting them. Rugby frames an essential piece of the national character of Wales, and the Welsh invest wholeheartedly in their capacity to ace this game. Other games that are prevalent are cricket and soccer.

Food and Drink

The menu depends for the most part on locally accessible items, including beef, mutton, and vegetables such as leeks, cabbages, and potatoes. Fish and seafood are also standard items. The cawl is viewed as the national dish and is a juice of meat (Beef or mutton) and vegetables. The Welsh rarebit is another claim to fame comprising of Toasted brezd finished with a mixture of liquefied cheddar, milk, eggs, and Worcestershire sauce. Brew and bourbon are crafted locally, though on a smaller scale than in England or Scotland.

Dress

Regularly, Western garments are worn. In celebrations, notwithstanding, ladies once in a while wear the customary national clothing, which wound up prominent during the nineteenth century. It comprises of a long skirt (usually red), a checkered cover, and a tall, dark cap. In rural areas, this clothing keeps on being seen among certain ladies.

Sports

Rugby is likely the most mainstream sport, having numerous passionate fans. Multiple individuals see it as a matter of national personality and pride, and the matches against England are frequently a significant occasion. Cricket and soccer are other famous games.

Political Life

Government.
The First Minister operates from Whitehall in London, the name of the authoritative and political seat of the British government. Increasing pressure from Welsh pioneers for more self-sufficiency acquired devolution of organization May 1999, implying that progressively political power was given to the Welsh Office in Cardiff. The situation of the secretary of state for Wales, a piece of the British head administrator's bureau, was made in 1964. In a 1979 submission a proposition for the making of a non-legislating Welsh Assembly was rejected but in 1997 another choice passed by a thin margin, prompting the 1998 production of the National Assembly for Wales. The Assembly has sixty individuals and is in charge of setting arrangement and making enactment in areas in regards to training, health, farming, transportation, and social administrations. A general revamping of government all through the United Kingdom in 1974 incorporated a simplification of Welsh organization with smaller regions regrouped to frame more prominent voting public for monetary and political reasons. Grains were rearranged into eight new areas, from thirteen originally, and inside the provinces, thirty-seven new areas made.

Leadership and Political Officials.
Wales has dependably had a solid left wing and radical ideological groups and pioneers. There is also stable political mindfulness all through Wales, and voter turnout at decisions is higher than in the United Kingdom. In a large portion of the nineteenth and mid-twentieth centuries, the Liberal Party ruled Welsh legislative issues with the new areas secondary to the Socialists. In 1925 the Welsh Nationalist Party, recognized as Plaid Cymru, was popular with the goal of earning freedom

for Wales as an area inside the European Economic Community. Between World Wars I and II extreme monetary depression caused just about 430,000 Welsh to move and another political activism brought into the world with an emphasis on social and financial change. After World War II the Labor Party picked up a more significant part of help. Plaid Cymru and the Conservative Gathering won places in political decisions, debilitating the Labor Party's customary

predominance of Welsh legal issues. During the 1970s and 1980s, Conservatives gained significantly more control, a pattern that was turned around during the 1990s with the arrival of Labor strength and the increased help for Plaid Cymru and Welsh patriotism. The Welsh rebel, patriot development also incorporates progressively radical gatherings who look for the making of a politically free country by social and phonetic changes. The Welsh Language Culture is one of the more unmistakable of these gatherings and has expressed its ability to use common insubordination to encourage its objectives.

Military Activity.
Wales does not have an autonomous military, and its protection falls to the army of the United Kingdom in general. However, there are three armed regiments that have strong ties to Wales: the Welsh Guards, the Royal Regiment of Wales, and the Royal Welch Fusiliers, that have strong associations with the nation.

Social Welfare and Change Programs

Health and social administrations fall under the organization and obligation of the secretary of state for Wales. The Welsh Office, which works with province and locale specialists, designs and executes matters identifying with housing, health, training, and welfare.

Horrible working and living conditions in the nineteenth century brought significant changes and new strategies concerning social welfare that continued being enhanced all through the twentieth century. Issues in regards to health care, lodging, training, and working conditions, joined with an abnormal state of political activism, have made a consciousness of and demand for social change programs in Wales.

Chapter 12: Gender Roles and Statuses

The Relative Status of Women and Men

Historically, Women had few rights, albeit many worked outside the home, and were required to satisfy the job of wife, mother, sometimes to the children of distant relatives. In agricultural areas women worked alongside male family members. When the Welsh economy started to industrialize, numerous women looked for employment in manufacturing plants that procured a solely female workforce for occupations not requiring physical effort. Women and childrens worked in mines, putting in fourteen-hour days under dangerous conditions. The enactment was passed in the mid-nineteenth century constraining the working hours for women and kids, but it was not until the start of the twentieth century that Welsh women started to demand Progressive social liberties. The Women's Institute, which currently has branches all through the United Kingdom, was established in Wales, albeit all of its exercises directed in English. During the 1960s another association, like the Women's Institute but solely Welsh in its objectives, was established. Known as the Merced y Wawr, or Women of the Dawn, it is committed to advancing the privileges of Welshwomen, the Welsh language and culture, and sorting out magnanimous undertakings.

Socialization

Tyke Rearing and Education. Children were abused in the name of work by being sent into mines in tubes that were too small for adults. Child and baby death rates were high: practically 50% of all kids did not live past the age of five, and just 50% of the individuals who lived past the age of ten were unlikely to live to their mid-twenties. Social reformers and religious associations, especially the Methodist Church, supported improved government funded training standards in the mid-nineteenth century. Conditions started to gradually improve for kids when working hours were limited and mandatory schooling established. The Education Act of 1870 was passed to implement basic standards, but also tried to oust Welsh totally from the School curriculum.

Today, essential and nursery schools in areas with a Welsh-speaking lion's share give guidance totally in Welsh and schools in zones where English is the primary language offer bilingual advice. The Welsh Language Nursery Schools Crusade, Mudiad Ysgolion Meithrin Cymraeg, originated in 1971 and has been extremely fruitful in making a system of nursery schools, or Ysgolion Meithrin, particularly in districts where English used as often as possible. Nursery, essential, and auxiliary schools are under the organization of the instruction expert of the Welsh Office. Quality government funded schooling is accessible all through Wales for understudies of any age.

Higher Education.

Most institutions of higher learning are publicly supported, but admission is competitive. The Welsh literary tradition, a high literacy rate, and political and religious factors have all contributed to shaping a culture where higher education is considered important. The primary organization of higher learning is the University of Wales, a state-funded college supported by the Universities Funding Council, with six areas in Wales: Aberystwyth, Lampeter, Cardiff, Swansea, Bangor, and the Welsh National School of Medicine. The Welsh Office is in charge of other colleges and schools, including the Polytechnic of Wales, close to Pontypridd, and the University College of Wales at Aberystwyth. The Welsh Office, employed with the Local Education Authorities and the Welsh Joint Education Committee, administers all aspects of government funded training. Grown-up proceeding with instruction courses, especially those in Welsh language and culture, are firmly advanced through local projects.

Religion

Religion has assumed a significant role in the molding of Welsh culture. Protestantism, and in particular, Anglicanism, started to accumulate more followers after Henry VIII destitute with the Roman Catholic Ecclesiastical. On the eve of the English Civil War in 1642, Puritanism, drilled by Oliver Cromwell and his supporters, was far-reaching in the fringe areas of Wales and Pembrokeshire. Welsh royalists who upheld the lord and Anglicanism were deprived of their property, acquiring disdain among non-Puritan Welsh. In 1650 the Act for the Spread of the Gospel in Wales was approved, taking over both political and spiritual life. During the period known as the Interregnum when Cromwell was in power, several non-Anglican, or

Dissenting, Protestant congregations were formed which were to have significant influences on modern Welsh life. The most dutifully and informally radical of these were the Quakers, who had substantial successes in Montgomeryshire and Merioneth and finally spread their impact to areas including the Anglican fringe districts and the Welsh-speaking regions in the north and west. The Quakers, actively disliked by both other Dissenting places of worship and the Anglican Church, were severely subdued with the outcome that huge numbers were compelled to emigrate to the American states. Different areas of prayer, for example, the Baptist and Congregationalist, which were Calvinist in religious philosophy, developed and found numerous supporters in small towns. In the last part of the eighteenth century, many Welsh converted to Methodism after a restoration development in 1735. Methodism was bolstered inside the setup Anglican Church and was initially sorted out through neighborhood social orders represented by a local association. The impact of the first Dissenting holy places, joined with the profound restoration of Methodism, gradually drove Welsh society far from Anglicanism. Clashes in the initiative and constant neediness made church development difficult, but the prevalence of Methodism eventually settled as the most far-reaching section. The Methodist and other Dissenting chapels were also in charge of an increase in proficiency through chapel supported schools that advanced instruction as a method for spreading religious principle.

Today, devotees of Methodism still establish the most significant religious gathering. The Anglican Church is the additional most significant order, trailed by the Roman Catholic Church. There are also smaller quantities of Jews and Muslims. The Dissenting Protestant sects, and religion in general, played very important roles in modern Welsh society but the number of people who regularly participated in religious activities dropped significantly after World War II.

Rituals

The Cathedral of Saint David in Pembrokeshire is an essential national holy spot. David, the benefactor saint of Wales, was a religious crusader who touched base in Wales in the 6th century to spread Christianity and convert the Welsh clans. He passed on in 589 on 1 March, presently celebrated as Saint David's Day, a national occasion. His remains are buried in the cathedral.

Medication and Health Care

Health care and drug are government-financed and upheld by the National Health Service of the United Kingdom. There is an exclusive expectation of health care in Wales with roughly six medical practitioners per ten thousand people. The Welsh National School of Medicine in Cardiff offers quality therapeutic preparing and instruction.

Common Celebrations

During the nineteenth century, Welsh intellectuals began to promote the national culture and traditions, initiating a revival of Welsh folk culture. In the last century, these festivals have developed into real occasions, and Wales currently has a few internationally important music and abstract celebrations. The most critical Welsh ordinary festival is the Eisteddfod social get-together commending music, verse, and narration.

The Eisteddfod had its starting points in the twelfth century when it was mostly a gathering held by Welsh troubadours for the trading of information. Occurring unpredictably and in different areas, the Eisteddfod was attended by writers, artists, and troubadours, all of whom had essential jobs in medieval Welsh culture. By the eighteenth century, the convention had turned out to be not so much social but rather tipsy bar gatherings, but in 1789 the Gwyneddigion Society restored the Eisteddfod as a focused celebration. It was Edward Williams, also recognized as Iolo Morgannwg, in any case, who stirred Welsh enthusiasm for the Eisteddfod in the nineteenth century. Williams effectively advanced the Eisteddfod among the Welsh people living in London, regularly giving emotional addresses about the significance of Welsh culture and old Celtic customs. The nineteenth century revival of the Eisteddfod and the rise of Welsh nationalism, combined with a romantic image of ancient Welsh history, led to the creation of Welsh ceremonies and rituals that may not have any historical basis.

The Llangollen Global Musical Eisteddfod is held from 4 to 9 July, and the Royal National Eisteddfod at Llanelli, which highlights a verse and Welsh society expressions, held from 5 to 12 August, are the two most essential mainstream festivities. Other smaller, society and social celebrations are held consistently.

Chapter 13: The Arts and Humanities

Support for the Arts

The conventional significance of music and verse has energized global support for all of the expressions of the human experience. There is strong public support throughout Wales for the arts, which are considered important to the national culture. Financial support is derived from both the private and public sectors. The Welsh Arts Council gives government assistance to writing, artistry, music, and theater. The committee also offers gifts to scholars to both English-and Welsh-language productions.

Literature

Literature and verse have involve a critical position in Wales. Welsh culture is based on an oral convention of legends, fantasies, and folktales passed down from age to age. Increased knowledge, in the eighteenth century and the worry of Welsh learned people for the safeguarding of the language and culture brought forth present day composed Welsh writing. As industrialization and Anglicization compromised common Welsh culture, endeavors were made to advance the word, safeguard Welsh verse, and empower Welsh scholars. Dylan Thomas was one such Welsh writer, and possibly the most famous in the twentieth century. Artistic celebrations and rivalries help keep this custom alive. Nevertheless, the influence of other cultures combined with the ease of communication through mass media, from both inside the United Kingdom and from other parts of the world, continually undermine efforts to preserve a purely Welsh form of literature.

Performance Arts.

Singing is the most important of the performance arts in Wales and has its roots in ancient traditions. Music was both diversion and methods for recounting stories. The Welsh National Opera is one of the leading musical show organizations in Britain. Wales is celebrated for its all-male choirs, which have developed from the religious choral convention. Customary instruments, for example, the harp, are still broadly played and since 1906, the Welsh Folk Song Society has safeguarded, gathered, and distributed familiar tunes. The Welsh Theater Company is critically acclaimed, and Wales has created numerous internationally Well-known on-screen characters.

Chapter 14: Description of significant historical places

Kidwelly Castle

If you want a genuinely medieval minute, look at Kidwelly Castle in [location] enveloped in an early morning fog. Spine-tingling stuff. It is up to par with any of the other incredible castles of Wales.

The Earliest Castle on the site was Norman and made of earth and timber. The town itself is equally antiquated, built around 1115 AD. When the thirteenth century had tagged along the castle had been remade in stone, after the half-moon shape taken by the Normans. The Chaworth family assembled the reduced, but amazing internal ward and the villa was later modified by the lords (eventually dukes) of Lancaster.

Kidwelly benefited from the latest thinking in castle design. It had a concentric plan with one circuit of cautious walls set inside another to allow the castle to hold regardless of whether the external wall should fall. The construction of the large gatehouse was started late in the fourteenth century, but it wasn't finished until 1422, thanks to some degree to Owain Glyn Dwr's endeavors to stop it going up.

As with any old structure, accessibility can be a problem, but the creation of a timber-surrounded footbridge, the first passage has become wheelchair-accessible in recent years. The construction revealed an unforeseen reward: a secret underground passage!

Cyfarthfa Castle Museum and Art Gallery

Cyfarthfa Castle situated in the authentic town of Merthyr Tydfil, which set up itself as the Iron Capital of the World in the Eighteenth Century with its large Iron-Works buildings.

Cyfarthfa Castle is an incredible outing, set on the edge of the pleasant Brecon Beacons National Park, with a coffee bar offering tasty food, and an outside seating zone, which is ideal for unwinding in the late spring months.

Cyfarthfa Castle arranged in 160 acres of land of parkland with formal gardens, a lake, childrens' play region, and a model railroad. The castle was built in 1824 during the industrial revolution, and has now opened its doors to the public, hosting a spectacular museum and art gallery. Guests can observe a scope of artistry presentations and mixed Trade goods from the old world, including Egyptian grave products, Greek and Roman artifacts and Far Eastern decorative arts.

The Six Bells Miners Memorial

Finished in 2010, Guardian was dispatched to commemorate the 50th anniversary of the 1960 mining disaster in Six Bells that killed 45 men. The stunning 20-meter towers over the site of the former colliery where the catastrophe happened and is an appropriate compliment to the men whose names cut into boards folded over the commemoration plinth.

- Designed by craftsman Sebastien Boyesen, the statue is built from more than 20,000 pieces of Corten steel welded together to form a landmark that stands proudly, on a sandstone plinth. The detail that has been made utilizing this unorthodox system allows for the facial highlights, muscle definition and hair to be noticeable, and even the trousers seem delicate and streaming.
- Viewed from a distance the figure of the miner has a transparent, almost ghostly quality, allowing it to blend into the heavily wooded landscape setting. Only when viewed up close, does the figure appear solid and the true presence of Guardian can be fully appreciated.
- Guardian was devoted as a component of a Commemoration Service on the 28th June 2010 driven by the Archbishop of Canterbury Reverend Rowan Williams, and later in November 2011, HRH Prince Charles visited Guardian and Ty Ebbw Fach.
- Ty Ebbw Fach has a heritage room detailing the history of Guardian, Six Bells Colliery and the village of Six Bells. It also houses a small café serving delicious, homemade hot and cold refreshments.
- Guardian sits in Parc Arael Griffin, one of 14 environmental sites on the Ebbw Fach Trail and three of the Tyleri Trails also start from this point.

Strata Florida Abbey (Cadw)

There is much to captivate at this evocative, historically important site. Is Latin Dutch to you? Strata Florida is Latin, and can be translated to mean the Vale of Flowers. In Welsh, the name is the Cistercian priests of the Middle Ages were incredible business plural. They may have looked for wild and desolate spots to rehearse their religion but, like anxious engineers, they took the preferred standpoint of this rural area near Tregaron to amass large measures of land. They needed the space to cultivate thousands of hyphenated sheep. They also assembled streets and scaffolds which connected explorers and merchants to the nunnery — a quick move.

Strata Florida rapidly wound up not just a site of enormous religious significance in Wales but also a private home for Welsh culture. Dafydd ap Gwilym, a standout amongst the best known about Wales' medieval artists, is covered here under a yew tree.

The gigantic west entryway conveys the former glory of the building. The plan of the church can still be clearly traced and, rather remarkably, some of the original richly decorated tiles from the abbey are still intact. One of them, 'Man with the Mirror,' delineates a medieval man appreciating himself in a mirror!

Oyster Mouth Castle

With staggering views over Mumbles, Oyster Mouth Castle sits majestically on the slope sitting above Swansea Bay. It's looking especially great nowadays because of an ongoing facelift. A large amount of work has resulted in the castle being lined with an overhead shelter, protecting it for years to come.

Earth has been dug under the expert eye of Glamorgan Gwent archaeologists to expose private staircases leading from vaults to previous banqueting halls. Stairs have helped by lime washing walls and made safe with rope handrails.

The Copper Kingdom Center, Amlwch

This new heritage visitor centre tells the story of Anglesey's former role as the world's leading copper producer. You can get the lowdown through intelligent presentations and exercises. In 2013, it was shortlisted for a Guardian Museum and Heritage Award for the UK's most moving museum or legacy guest fascination.

The "Copper Kingdom" alludes to the region of Amlwch on Anglesey, North Wales, which once had the biggest copper mine on the planet.

Caerphilly Castle

Caerphilly, covering 30 acres of land (12.2ha), is one of the best enduring castles in the medieval Western world. It was a highpoint in medieval protective engineering with its massive gatehouses and water highlights. It was created by Earl Gilbert de Clare, starting in 1268, to frighten Llywelyn, the last native Prince of Wales, from fighting the Normans in the southern part of Wales. It then used as a model for Edward I's castles in North Wales. Cunning Llywelyn caught it when it was half completed, but it was before long back in Norman's hands.

After Llywelyn's defeat and death, the Welsh threat substantially ended, and the castle became the administrative centre for de Clare's estates. Edward II invested energy here. Caerphilly, being uncomfortable for a family residence, eventually rotted, and the stone was taken to assemble an adjacent country house. The Victorian Bute family coal cash protected and reestablished the castle. An informative Castles of Wales exhibition is located in one tower. Working replicas of attack motors are on the grounds. There is an AV visit accessible.

Blaenavon has a pretty fantastic story

Blaenavon is a town that has throughout history been largely reliant on its coal industry. With the Great Depression and a post-war decreased need for coal, the economy was devastated. But starting with a state pledge to protect Blaenavon's Ironworks during the 1970s – the famous 18th century furnaces are attracting record visitor numbers these days. The town has appreciated a proper restoration, coming full circle in its acknowledgment as a World Heritage Site at the turn of the thousand years.

The judges had heaps of reasons to esteem Blaenavon deserving of Inclusion with the likes of the Taj Mahal and The Great Wall of China: each step taken shadows living history. The choice to give the town protection status in 1984 has paid off, keeping a significant number of the well-established niches, crevices and cobbled ways around old structures around the enchanting and suggestive Broad Street.

The pedestrianized areas make it significantly easier to sample nearby food and drink – a tempting prospect given the scope of cheddar, bread, meats and rarities created in the town.

Where mines, collieries, cable cars and prepares once overwhelmed the landscape, wildlife and vegetation have now returned in health.

Cyclists can whizz along the previous mineral railroad line, which presently frames a bicycle course driving the path to a portion of the attractions.

Huge Pit, the National Coal Mining Museum, is a standout amongst the most suggestive legacy settings on the planet, paying tribute to the sweat and effort of excavators grind of miners through a blacksmith's forge, a miners' canteen and an explosive magazine. You'll be able to imagine hard-hatters using the lockers and shower rooms, kept intact at a place which has won multiple awards and, amazingly, is free of charge.

Another must-see is the Workmen's Hall, a monumental stone building which has gone about as an active point of convergence for the nearby network since 1895. It's also well worth visiting the World Heritage Center, where a program incorporates intuitive shows and expressions and artworks exercises for the children.

Truth be told, Blaenavon is an extraordinary destination in any season, from the blossoms of spring to summer days following the Iron Mountain Trail. The yearly Winter Wonderland in December, when the Heritage Railway – moving at the greatest height of any saved household railroad, driven by a devoted group of enthusiasts – runs a Santa Special administration.

Sun-kissed or chilly, incredible undertakings await the guest.

Chapter 15: Welsh Key Figures

Roald Dahl

Roald Dahl was a well-known British essayist and author of cunning, humorous children's books. He was born 13 September, 1916 in Llandaff, Wales.

Following his graduation from Repton, an eminent British government funded school, in 1932, Dahl decided against from college and joined an undertaking to Newfoundland. He served from 1937 to 1939 in Dar es Salaam, Tanganyika (presently in Tanzania), but he enrolled in the Royal Air Force (RAF) when World War II broke out. Flying as a military pilot, he was injured in a crash landing in Libya. He presented with his squadron in Greece and then in Syria before completing a stretch (1942– 43) as assistant air attaché in Washington, D.C. (during which time he also filled in as a covert agent for the British government). There the author C.S. Forester urged him to expound on his most energizing RAF experiences, which were distributed by the Saturday Evening Post.

Dahl's first book, The Gremlins (1943), was composed for Walt Disney but was to a great extent unsuccessful. His administration in the RAF influenced his first story release, Over to You: Ten Stories of Flyers and Flying (1946), a progression of military stories that was energetically bought by critics but did not sell well. He accomplished smash hit status with Somebody Like You (1953), a gathering of grim stories for grown-ups, which was followed by Kiss, Kiss (1959), which focused on sentimental connections.

Dahl at that point swung principally to composing the children's books that would give him lasting distinction. Unlike most books that went for a youthful gathering of people, Dahl's works had an obscurely funny nature, every now and again including grisly viciousness and demise. His Characters were frequently malignant grown-ups who endangered bright and honorable tyke heroes. James and the Giant Peach (1961; film 1996), composed for his Own children, was a prominent achievement. His different works for young perusers incorporate Fantastic Mr. Fox, Charlies and the Chocolate Factory, and the Great Glass Elevator, The Enormous Crocodile, The BFG, and The Witches. One of his last such books, Matilda, was adapted as a film and as a stage show.

Dahl also composed a few contents for motion pictures, among them You Only Live Twice and Chitty Bang. His collection of memoirs, Boy: Tales of Childhood, was distributed in 1984.

Aneurin Bevan

In Tredegar, Wales, Aneurin Bevan was born in 1897, 15th November. His dad was a coal digger and the poor regular workers family in which Bevan grew up gave him direct experience to the issues of poverty and disease.

Bevan left school at 13 and started working in a neighborhood colliery. He turned into an exchanges association extremist and won a grant to examine in London. It was during this period that he wound up persuaded by the ideas of communism. During the 1926 General Strike, Bevan became one of the pioneers of the South Wales mineworkers. In 1929, Bevan was chosen as the Labor individual from parliament for Ebbw Vale.

During World War Two, Bevan was one of the leaders of the left in the House of Commons. After the landslide Labor triumph in the 1945 general decision, Bevan was selected priest of health, in charge of building up the National Health Service. On 5 July 1948, the legislature took over duty regarding all medicinal administrations, and there were free analysis and treatment for all.

Aneurin Bevan was a standout amongst the most critical pastors of the post-war Labor government and the central modeler of the National Health Service.

In 1951, Bevan was moved to become minister of labour. In an immediately afterward, he left the administration in the challenge at the presentation of remedial charges for dental consideration and displays. Bevan drove the left wing of the Labor Party, known as the 'Bevanites,' for the following five years. He arose as one of the applicants for gathering pioneer in 1955 but was defeat by Hugh Gaitskell. He consented to fill in as remote shadow secretary under Gaitskell.

In 1959, Bevan was chosen appointee pioneer of the Labor Party, although he was at that point experiencing malignant terminal cancer. He died on 6 July 1960.

Richard Burton

Richard Burton: history

In 2002, Richard Burton was incorporated into the list of the best British in history, alongside Charles Darwin, John Lennon, Sir Winston Churchill, Princess Diana, and others. The seven-time Academy Award winner, Richard Burton was the most renowned and generously compensated actor during the 1960s.

Childhood

He was born in 1925, 10th November, in the Welsh town Pontrhydyfen into large family. His father was a coal digger and his mother a [profession] married in [year] and together had thirteen children, of which Richard was the twelfth. His mother passed away in labor with his youngest sibling, when Richard was around two years old. Afterward, the family lived in poverty and could barely make ends meet.

The last on-screen character's youth can scarcely be called natural. his father spent what he earned on liquor and betting. Richard's senior sister Cecilia and her husband Elfed James, also a coalminer, took him [and his siblings] in. Afterward, Richard considered his Sister's help fortunately and stated:

> "She felt all catastrophes except her own."

Cecilia took the mother's place for the more youthful sibling. The senior sibling Ifor also contributed to the craftsman's childhood: he ingrained the affection for rugby in the child.

At five, Richard began attending the Eastern Primary School in Neath Port Talbot. After three years, he transferred to another school. The future star demonstrated the adoration for authorship in his adolescence; he had a beautiful voice and cherished the English and Welsh writing.

Motion pictures

Richard's teacher Philip Burton turned into a significant figure in Jenkins' life. It's his second name that the young fellow took as a piece of his stage name. The instructor saw the skilled understudy and supported his passion for theater. Philip helped a young Richard improve his discourse and talk without an accent.

Richard Burton in the motion picture My Cousin Rachel

In 1948, Richard Burton debuted in the motion picture The Last Days of Dolwyn. Before, the performing artist had been dealing with the radio for quite a while and also played in the theater.

The dramatization My Cousin Rachel was the artist's Hollywood debut in 1952. The motion picture turned out to be one of Henry Koster's best ventures.

Richard Burton in the motion picture The Taming of the Shrew

Richard Burton was nominated for the Academy Award multiple times, but he never got the hotly anticipated prize. In 1970, the ruler of the western John Wayne picked up his award and saw Richard had none. He murmured to Richard that Burton merited the honor.

The individual life of the gifted and handsome performing artist was as productive as his filmography. The man was married multiple times: Sybil Williams, Susan Hunt, Sally Hay, and Elizabeth Taylor (twice).

Sybil Williams Gave birth to two of Burton's Daughters, Kate and Jessica.

The undertaking between Richard and Elizabeth Taylor was a standout amongst the most scandalous and broadly examined news. The entire world was viewing the narrative of the star couple, and the actors did not keep it's a subtleties mystery.

Burton's accomplice in the motion picture Cleopatra (and twelve different works) turned into his extraordinary love. Richard got down to business on the motion picture and took his family. In any case, nothing could keep the sentiment from creating.

Elizabeth and Richard wedded in March 1964. Right then and there, Burton was the most generously compensated performer in Hollywood, and Elizabeth was the ruler of shooting.

Their life was like a fantasy: lavish yachts, relics, land property. The performing artists gave each other costly shows. Their fans viewed the passionate couple for a long time. Eventually, they separated. Even though Elizabeth and Richard remarried in some time, they lived respectively for not exactly a year. In their meetings, the stars admitted they cherished one another but couldn't exist together.

Demise
The performer passed away at an early age (58). As indicated by his biographers, Richard became liquor subordinate in his childhood, and the propensity changed into fixation later. Also, the craftsman was a smoker.

The performer was 58 when he died abruptly. It occurred in Céligny, Geneva, Switzerland, where he had a house.

Filmography
1953 – The Desert Rats

1955 – Prince of Players

1959 – Look Back in Anger

1962 – The Longest Day

1963 – Cleopatra

1964 – The Night of the Iguana

1967 – Doctor Faustus

1972 – Bluebeard

1977 – Exorcist II: The Heretic

1978 – The Wild Geese

King Arthur Biography

Lord Arthur is a semi-legendary figure, who is accepted to have been a model ruler in the early history of Britain. Much of his early legend comes from the writings of Geoffrey of Monmouth (in the Twelfth Century). His works became popular, cementing the legend of Arthur in popular folklore. All through the ages, the figure of Arthur has enthralled the enthusiasm of journalists and artists. Alfred Tennyson was instrumental in resuscitating interest for King Arthur through his ballad, "Idylls of the King."

Because of the absence of legitimate and direct chronicled proof, the life of King Arthur is available to a wide range of elucidations. A few historians question whether he truly existed at all. Notwithstanding, the most acclaimed legends incorporate the accompanying stories.

Birth to Uther Pendragon and Igraine
In one rendition, Merlin prophesized that a future king named Arthur would be born to Uther Pendragon and Igraine, the beautiful wife of Duke Gorlois of Cornwall. Knowing she would reject a man other than her husband, Uther asked Merlin to enable him to lay down with Igraine. Merlin obliged, transforming Uther's appearance to resemble the Duke for one night.

Excalibur
As indicated by legend, Arthur was ready to guarantee his rightful spot as King of Britain when he pulled Excalibur, a legendary sword, from the stone. When he obtained the sword, he fulfilled his prophecy and was crowned king. All through his rule, Arthur was advised by the slippery and mysterious figure of Merlin. Until the sixth century, it was reasonable for Welsh Kings to have an advisor, regularly called "Murthur." These

guides frequently had specific data and were knowledgeable in expressions of the human experience of divination. The legend of Merlin is likely based on these court guides.

King Arthur Court
The court of Arthur kept up the most astounding standards of gallantry and ethical conduct. Furthermore, Arthur wished for his chosen knights to sit around a round table so that nobody would be superior. He tried to treat all as equal. Knights of King Arthur included:

- Sir Kay,
- Sir Gawain,
- Sir Lancelot,
- Sir Percival
- Sir Galahad,
- Sir Tristan
- Sir Bors
- Sir Geraint
- Sir Gareth
- Sir Lamorak
- Sir Gaheris
- Sir Bedivere
- Sir Agravaine
- Sir Sagramore

King Arthur and Lady Guinevere
In spite of the high requirements of honor one legend tells how one of King Arthur's most trusted and effective knights, Sir Lancelot took part in an extramarital entanglement with Arthur's wife, Queen Guinevere. It was this betrayal that ultimately led to King Arthur's downfall.

Lord Arthur and the Holy Grail
A standout amongst the most enduring legends of King Arthur is the enchanted mission for the blessed chalice. this is a

container used to catch the blood of Jesus Christ. For some, the purpose of the Holy Chalice is an allegory of the profound internal journey to find the elusive purpose of life. This fantasy has enraptured the enthusiasm of individuals through the ages and has been the subject of numerous movies including the sarcastic Monty Python and the Holy Grail.

Ruler Arthur and Mordred

All through Arthur's missions, he is opposed Morgan le Fay and Mordred. Records differ, but the most prevalent claims that Morgan le Fay was his stepsister and Mordred was his child.

T.E. Lawrence Biography

Military Leader (1888– 1935)
T.E. Lawrence was a British armed officer who Played the part in the Great Arab Revolt and later composed the journal The Seven Pillars of Wisdom.

List
T.E. Lawrence helped in the British military, getting to be Involved in Middle Eastern issues. He was a staunch promoter for Arab autonomy. later sought after a private life, changing his name. he passed on May 19, 1935.

'Lawrence of Arabia'
Born on August 16, 1888, in Tremadoc, Caernarvonshire, Wales, Thomas Edward Lawrence became an expert in Arab affairs as a junior archaeologist in Carchemish on the Euphrates River from 1911 to 1914, working for the British Museum on archaeological excavations. After the commencement of World War-I, he entered British knowledge.

Lawrence joined Amir Faisal al Husayn's rebel against the Turks as the political contact officer, driving a guerilla crusade that harassed the Turks behind their lines. After a significant triumph at Aqaba—a port city on the southern coast of what is presently Jordan—Lawrence's powers bolstered British General Allenby's battle to catch Jerusalem.

Catch
In 1917, T.E. Lawrence was caught at Dar'a and tormented and sexually abused, leaving scars that never mended. By 1918, Lawrence had been elevated to lieutenant colonel and granted the Illustrious Facility Order and the Instruction of Bath by King George V, but but politely refused the medals in support of Arab independence.

Spiritually and physically depleted, and Uneasy with his notoriety, Lawrence came back to England and began diligently working on an account of his adventures.

The Seven Pillars of Wisdom and Later Years
The Seven Pillars of Wisdom is one of his books, and it became known for its distinctive portrayals of the mind-boggling expansiveness and assortment of Lawrence's escapades in Arabia. The work accumulated universal distinction for Lawrence, who was appropriately nicknamed "Lawrence of Arabia."

After the war, Lawrence linked the Royal Air Force under an unexpected name, T.E. Shaw (as he continued looking for obscurity, he had his name officially changed).

Lawrence died in a cruiser mishap on May 19, 1935, in Clouds Hill, Dorset, England.

A movie based on his life, Lawrence of Arabia, coordinated by David Lean and featuring Peter O'Toole, was released in 1962. The film earned seven Academy Awards, plus the Oscar for best picture.

Conclusion

It seems that the progress of Welsh nationalism rallied supporters of the language, and the formation of Welsh television and radio originate a form of spectators which fortified in the retention of its Welsh. Maybe most important of all, at the end of the 20th century it became required for all schoolchildren to absorb Welsh up to age 16, and this both reinforced the language in Welsh-speaking areas and reintroduced at least a basic knowledge of it in the regions which had become more or less solely Anglophone.

The failure in the fraction of people in Wales who can express Welsh has now stopped, and there are even ciphers of a modest rescue. However, though Welsh is the daily language in many parts of Wales, English is universally understood. Additional, overall figures may be misleading, and it might argue that the mass of Welsh speakers (which, if high, leads to a flourishing Welsh philosophy) is a similarly important statistic. Put additional way, were 50,000 other Welsh speakers to be focused in areas where Welsh spoke by at least 50% of the populace, this would be much more significant to the sustainability of the Welsh language than the similar number discrete in Cardiff, Newport and Swansea cities.

With that, we have come to the end of this book. I want to thank you for choosing this book.

Now that you have come to the end of this book, we would first like to express our gratitude for choosing this particular source and taking the time to read through it. All the information here was well researched and put together in a way to help you understand the history of wales as easily as possible.

We hope you found it useful and you can now use it as a guide anytime you want. You may also want to recommend it to any family or friends that you think might find it useful as well.

www.ingramcontent.com/pod-product-compliance
Lightning Source LLC
Chambersburg PA
CBHW052202110526
44591CB00012B/2051